A PARENT'S GUIDE TO TEEN FOMO

A PARENT'S GUIDE TO

TEEN FOMO

axis

Tyndale House Publishers
Carol Stream, Illinois

Visit Tyndale online at tyndale.com.

Visit Axis online at axis.org.

Tyndale and Tyndale's quill logo are registered trademarks of Tyndale House Ministries.

A Parent's Guide to Teen FOMO

Copyright © 2022 by Axis. All rights reserved.

Cover illustration by Lindsey Bergsma. Copyright © Tyndale House Ministries. All rights reserved.

Designed by Lindsey Bergsma

For information about special discounts for bulk purchases, please contact Tyndale House Publishers at csresponse@tyndale.com, or call 1-800-323-9400.

Library of Congress Cataloging-in-Publication Data

A catalog record for this book is available from the Library of Congress.

ISBN 978-1-4964-6714-0

Printed in the United States of America

28	27	26	25	24	23	22
7	6	5	4	3	2	1

I believe that in all men's lives
at certain periods, and in many
men's lives at all periods between
infancy and extreme old age, one of
the most dominant elements is the
desire to be inside the local Ring and
the terror of being left outside. . . .
Unless you take measures to prevent
it, this desire is going to be one
of the chief motives of your life.

**C. S. LEWIS,
"THE INNER RING"**

CONTENTS

A LETTER FROM AXIS

Dear Reader,

We're Axis, and since 2007, we've been creating resources to help connect parents, teens, and Jesus in a disconnected world. We're a group of gospel-minded researchers, speakers, and content creators, and we're excited to bring you the best of what we've learned about making meaningful connections with the teens in your life.

This parent's guide is designed to help start a conversation. Our goal is to give you enough knowledge that you're able to ask your teen informed questions about their world. For each guide, we spend weeks reading, researching, and interviewing parents and teens in order to distill everything you need to know about the topic at hand. We encourage you to read the whole thing and then to use the questions we include to get the conversation going with your teen—and then to follow the conversation wherever it leads.

As Douglas Stone, Bruce Patton, and Sheila Heen point out in their book *Difficult Conversations*, "Changes in attitudes and behavior rarely come about because of arguments, facts, and attempts to persuade. How often do *you* change your values and beliefs—or whom you love or what you want in life—based on something someone tells you? And how likely are you to do so when the person who is trying to change you doesn't seem fully aware of the reasons you see things differently in the first place?"[1] For whatever reason, when we believe that others are trying to understand *our* point of view, our defenses usually go down, and we're more willing to listen to *their* point of view. The rising generation is no exception.

So we encourage you to ask questions, to listen, and then to share your heart with your teen. As we often say at Axis, discipleship happens where conversation happens.

Sincerely,
Your friends at Axis

---

[1] Douglas Stone, Bruce Patton, and Sheila Heen, *Difficult Conversations: How to Discuss What Matters Most*, rev. ed. (New York: Penguin Books, 2010), 137.

THE ONLY THING WE HAVE TO FEAR IS FOMO ITSELF.

IMAGINE YOURSELF as a teenager again. Try to remember some of the experiences, thoughts, and feelings you had. Do any of the following scenarios ring a bell?

1. You heard all about the excitement that went down at a party that you weren't invited to.

2. Your friends planned a fun trip, but you couldn't go.

3. You opted not to go to a movie with friends and ended up sitting at home wondering what you were missing.

4. It seemed that *everyone* in school was whispering about something, but you had no idea what it was.

5. Your summer vacation was boring and uneventful, so much so that you sat around envisioning all the

exciting things everyone else from school was doing.

The desire not to be left out is universal: no one *wants* to miss out on something interesting or important. This desire, which is especially strong during adolescence, stems from a God-given yearning to participate in significant experiences and be in meaningful community. So while it's a natural human tendency to fear being excluded, it's unhealthy when we let this fear control our lives.

Rather than getting easier, it's only gotten harder to resist feeling left out in today's world. The smartphone and social media have (perhaps intentionally) exploited this fear, making it even easier to see each and every little thing that happens without us. It's become such a powerful phenomenon that it's been given its own term: FOMO, the "fear of missing out."

FOMO is the worry that something interesting or exciting will happen without us, causing us to miss not just the experience but also the camaraderie that inevitably blossoms out of sharing it with others. Unfortunately, FOMO is a broken way of dealing with our God-given desires to live purposeful lives and be in community. God did not intend for us to live in a constant state of fear! Reclaiming our own boundaries and helping our kids reclaim theirs is well within our grasp, but it does require diligence, wisdom, and intentionality.

FOMO is the worry that something interesting or exciting will happen without us, causing us to miss not just the experience but also the camaraderie that inevitably blossoms out of sharing it with others.

WHERE DID THE TERM FOMO COME FROM?

WHILE PEOPLE HAVE ALWAYS wanted to be included, the acronym FOMO is relatively new. From what we can tell, marketing strategist Dan Herman gets the honor of being the person to coin the term. He says he first observed the phenomenon in the '90s and that approximately 70% of all adults in developed countries experience FOMO to various degrees.[1]

But it was Harvard Business School student Patrick McGinnis who really popularized it. In 2004 (when Facebook was barely a blip on the radar), he wrote a fairly popular article in which he described how FOMO was impacting the social lives of his fellow students, giving them an inability to commit to going to events because they feared they would miss a better opportunity.[2]

McGinnis wrote that FOMO has a close relationship with FOBO ("fear of a better option") and leads to FODA ("fear of doing anything"). He now says that the article was intended to be satirical, but (prophetically) ended up describing a mentality that has only increased exponentially thanks to the advent and widespread adoption of social media. He says:

> I've seen it grow from a strange quirk among my Harvard Business School classmates to something that has taken over every single area of our lives. We're always tempted by messages demanding us to try the hottest new trend, download the latest app, and, in the process, derail our goals to do something we don't really want to do out of the fear that if we don't try it, we're out of the conversation.[3]

WHY IS IT SO POWERFUL?

FOMO HAS SUCH A HOLD ON US because of two underlying principles. First, it's built on exclusivity (i.e., that there is an exclusive group of people who will enrich our lives in all the right ways if we can be part of it). In an article advising marketers on how to leverage Gen Z's FOMO, *HuffPost* writer Deep Patel observes, "Exclusivity is what feeds FOMO."[4]

Second, FOMO is based on the idea that there is always something—an activity, a gathering, an event, etc.—going on that we don't want to miss.

Combining the two is deadly. It keeps us constantly wondering, *What if?* and never able to be fully present or involved in what's happening. It's also a huge driver in smartphone addiction: *If I just scroll a bit farther, then maybe I'll see the right post. If I just keep watching YouTube vids a little longer, then I'll see the video that everyone will be talking about tomorrow.* . . . When the number of posts and videos is virtually infinite, it's easy to see how this can be paralyzing.

HOW IS IT AFFECTING US?

WE'RE ALWAYS LOOKING for that greener grass. If you search for entertainment news headlines containing "FOMO," you'll see a lot of jokes about it along the lines of "These Snapshots of Celebrities Will Give You the Worst FOMO, Haha!" The idea, of course, is that the lives of celebrities are so glamorous that you'll wish your life could be that exciting. However, Justin Bieber once posted on Instagram encouraging people not to be deceived by the false realities they see there—specifically how wonderful celebrities' lives seem.

FOMO has always existed in some form or another. One woman we talked to grew up in the '90s (i.e., before social media) and says that she used to be dominated by the fear that her friends were spending time together without her. She would constantly check AIM (that's AOL Instant Messenger, for those of you who might not remember) to see if her friends were online. If they weren't, she assumed they were doing something cool and fun but intentionally hadn't invited her. Another woman we talked to remembers that when she was a teen, her friend told her that whenever she was listening to one radio station, she felt like she must be missing out on a better song on a different station. (This was also in the '90s, before smartphones made music choices practically limitless.)

WE DON'T COMMIT.

One of the most recognizable symptoms of FOMO is the tendency, particularly of younger people, not to commit to anything. They are reluctant to commit to social events and might back out at the last minute, even if they said they were going to come. This happens with almost any big decision: where to go to college, whom to marry, or what job to take. Many young adults are scared that if they commit to a decision in one of these areas, they will make the wrong choice and miss out on a better option. Researchers even suggest that because of FOMO, employers will need to consider offering the members of Gen Z jobs where they can play multiple roles so that they can feel like they're not missing out on anything.[5]

OR WE OVERCOMMIT.

FOMO can also lead people to *overcommit*. Sometimes people are so afraid of missing out on something that they decide to do everything their friends invite them to—and then they run themselves ragged. This is how one man we talked to lived while he was in college. He tried to be part of every group he could and ended up exhausted from lack of sleep.

Researchers even suggest that because of FOMO, employers will need to consider offering the members of Gen Z jobs where they can play multiple roles so that they can feel like they're not missing out on anything.

Another woman we interviewed also used to try to make every possible social event and would never reject an invitation. The result was that she'd give away shifts at work, stay up late doing homework, and overdraft on her bank account. She stopped when she finally realized that the stress wasn't worth the financial cost or the toll on her quality of life.

WE OVERSPEND.

Credit Karma did a study on millennials and found that FOMO was a significant factor in their problem with overspending. Calling the problem "FOMO spending," the writers say that close to 40% of millennials overspend because they don't want to miss out on activities with their friends. According to these writers, "36% spend money they don't have because they're afraid they won't be included in a future activity if they don't."[6] (Keep in mind that unless your kids were born before 1996, they are Gen Zers, not millennials. So it remains to be fully seen if Gen Z will continue the trend of FOMO spending or if they'll push back against it for some reason.)

WE DON'T GIVE PEOPLE OUR FULL ATTENTION.

It's not just teens (Gen Zers) and millennials who are affected by trying to do everything at once. In her book *Alone Together*, MIT professor Sherry Turkle describes going to a conference where very few attendees were actually paying attention to the lectures. Rather, they were all multitasking on their devices.[7]

HOW DOES SOCIAL MEDIA RELATE TO FOMO?

SOCIAL MEDIA DOESN'T *CAUSE* FOMO, but it certainly does a lot to make it worse. In fact, it's not a stretch to say that social media may be the main conduit for FOMO these days. For example, many people recognize that they struggle with comparing their lives to the lives of others on TikTok or Instagram. Even though most of us realize on some level that we are looking at skewed depictions of reality (i.e., typically someone only posts their highlights to social media), we often have a hard time not comparing our everyday lives to these highlights and feeling bad about ourselves as a result. A teenage reader wrote into the *New York Times* with this concern about TikTok:

> As a teen, TikTok creates stress
> in my life. When I hang out with
> friends, they often ask if I want to

Social media doesn't *cause* FOMO, but it certainly does a lot to make it worse.

make a TikTok with them. I never suggest it, but it nearly always comes up. I want to be nice and say yes, but then I worry that other friends will see the clip and feel excluded that they weren't part of it. At times, TikToks have made me feel separate from my friends, and I don't want to make anyone else feel that.[8]

There could be many reasons for how social media increases our FOMO, but one we've observed is that it makes us more acutely aware of the things we're missing. Being finite and only able to do so much is part of being human. Every person in all of history has had to deal with this reality. What's different now is that *everything* we're missing—not just what our friends are doing without us, but what anyone in the world is doing without us—is unceasingly on display right in front of our faces via social media. So it's our *awareness* of what we're missing out on that has exponentially increased, not our actual inability to participate in everything. Maybe sometimes ignorance *is* bliss?

WHAT TRIGGERS IT?

1. WE'RE ALREADY INSECURE OR DEPRESSED.

Evidence suggests that some people experience FOMO worse than others do because they're already lonely, depressed, or discontent: "Those with low levels of satisfaction of the fundamental needs for competence, autonomy, and related-ness tend towards higher levels of fear of missing out as do those with lower levels of general mood and overall life satisfaction."[9]

2. WE SIMPLY HEAR ABOUT SOMETHING AWESOME.

One interesting finding from the research was that people feel FOMO just as in-tensely when they hear about something cool from a friend as when they hear about it via social media.[10] Even if people enjoyed the experience they chose, hear-ing about one they missed always made them feel bad. College students may be more vulnerable to FOMO because they feel like they have to maximize their time in college ("These are the best years of your life!").[11]

3. WE HAVE AN OVERWHELMING NUMBER OF CHOICES.

Another major factor contributing to FOMO is the sheer number of choices we face as the result of living in an affluent country. When it comes to the topic of how people are paralyzed by the inability to make decisions, probably no other person has been more cited than Barry Schwartz (he first published his book *The Paradox of Choice* in 2004). In his TED talk on the subject [*warning: there's a drawing of a topless woman at one point*], Schwartz says most of us have a deeply held belief that an increased number of choices will lead to greater freedom in our lives because we will have more opportunities. *But the opposite is actually true.* More choices lead not to greater freedom, but to higher levels of stress as we find it more difficult to narrow down our options. Because we have more to choose from, we are more likely to feel as though we missed out on something better.

Another fascinating aspect that Schwartz points out is that having more options *does make it possible for us to make objectively better decisions.* The only problem is that we're less happy with those decisions! He describes what it's like now for him to shop for a pair of jeans. While all the choices mean that he gets a pair of jeans that are of an objectively better quality than what he used to buy, he ironically feels worse about what he ends up with. And what makes all of these choices possible is the material wealth of the society in which we live.[12]

Because we have more to choose from, we are more likely to feel as though we missed out on something better.

HOW DOES IT AFFECT US LONG-TERM?

IT SEEMS THAT WHEN YOUNG people let FOMO control them, they tend to be more reckless on social media. Because of FOMO, "social media users may connect with more people on social media, post and update their social media platforms more frequently, and disclose more information about themselves and their activities with the public."[13] As you might expect, the more people put themselves out there on social media, the more opportunity they give to others who might want to bully or manipulate them. The more they post and look at posts on social media, the more likely it is that doing so will interfere with their real-life relationships.

One study found FOMO to be common among college freshmen. According to the study, those who frequently experienced it also dealt with "fatigue, stress, physical symptoms, and decreased sleep."[14] An article from Science Daily lists anxiety and depression as consequences of FOMO.[15]

Beyond that, it affects our hearts and minds too. More on that next.

WHY DOES GEN Z EXPERIENCE IT SO INTENSELY?

SOCIAL MEDIA—AND HOW accessible smartphones have made it—is probably the most significant reason why Gen Z has such a problem with FOMO. *HuffPost* reports:

> Nearly 90% of members of Gen Z use Snapchat on a regular basis, and a majority check Snapchat over 10 times a day, according to one study. Why are Gen Zers checking Snapchat so obsessively? It's because they don't want to miss out on what their friends are sharing.[16]

In fact, keeping up with everything on social media is getting so burdensome to the members of Gen Z that many of them are getting off social media because of the negative impact it's having on their lives.[17]

Comedian and actor Aziz Ansari points out [*warning: strong language, but still very insightful*] that one reason why young people have a hard time committing to spending time together is that they are always connected to their friends through technology.[18] The result is that seeing a friend face-to-face is not as special as it used to be. Even phone calls, which used to be more of an "event," are not a priority for young people anymore.

In fact, keeping up with everything on social media is getting so burdensome to the members of Gen Z that many of them are getting off social media because of the negative impact it's having on their lives.

HOW DO I HELP MY KIDS VIEW FOMO THROUGH THE LENS OF SCRIPTURE?

GOD'S WORD OFTEN SEEMS irrelevant to Gen Z because they don't think it has anything to say about their modern-day interests or struggles. If your teens are struggling with or being ruled by FOMO, it's a perfect opportunity to lovingly demonstrate Scripture's relevance and, in so doing, disciple them into a deeper understanding of God, themselves, others, and their world.

NO FEAR!

It's possible that calling it "FOMO" distracts us from what it actually is: fear. We all need to be reminded that God has given us "a spirit not of fear but of power and love and self-control" (2 Timothy 1:7). In fact, one of the most repeated commands in all of Scripture is "Do not be afraid."[19] We are to live from a place of knowing God's love for us and loving our neighbors as ourselves. But that's much easier said than done, especially when you're a teenager in today's world, which we'll talk more about below.

FOMO = IDOLATRY.

Anytime we want something so much that we'll do *anything* for it (even and especially ignoring God's plans and desires for us), we're guilty of idolatry. Isn't that exactly what we're doing when we allow FOMO to control our schedules and consume our thoughts? We either idolize ourselves ("*I* have a hard time committing because *I* am afraid *I* won't have the best experience *I* could") or we idolize experiences. Either way, it's all about taking control into our own hands to make our lives the best they can be, regardless of how that impacts others. In the end, what we're basically communicating to others and to God is that we know best, that we

It's possible that calling it "FOMO" distracts us from what it actually is: fear.

can do better with our time and our lives than God Himself can (sounds a lot like a certain couple in a certain garden . . . not naming any names, though).

Whoa. For most teens, learning to see this root of the issue can be mind-blowing. They may even deny it for a while. But give it time to sink in. Once it does, your teens may be overwhelmed with guilt and shame, just like the "garden couple." If so, it helps to remind them that every human in all of history is guilty of idolatry to some degree—it's a sin that's been passed down since the Garden of Eden, one that won't be eradicated until Christ renews heaven and earth. It also helps to remind them that through Christ we have the power to overcome, resting in the relief that God really does know best and desires *even more than we do* for us to live abundant lives.

HOW WE HANDLE FOMO SPEAKS TO OUR INTEGRITY.

To *never* commit to anything or to *always* go back on our commitments is disrespectful to the people who have made the plans and invited us. We're not saying there shouldn't be grace if someone has to miss an event now and then. But overall, we should have a general pattern of doing what we say we will do. Jesus said, "Let what you say be simply 'Yes' or 'No'; anything more than this comes from evil" (Matthew 5:37). In other words, it demonstrates that we lack integrity.

GOD LOVES US FAR MORE THAN WE LOVE OURSELVES.

We've probably all experienced going to an event that we were excited about and then ending up being disappointed. So how are teens to combat the anxiety they feel about missing out on something cool or going to something that seems like it will be cool and being let down? Several truths can help us here. One is that we can bring all of our anxieties to God and know that He is more than capable of taking care of them. Philippians 4:6-7 says,

Do not be anxious about anything, but in everything by prayer and supplication with thanksgiving let your requests be made known to God. And the peace of God, which surpasses all understanding, will guard your hearts and your minds in Christ Jesus.

Paul tells us that we don't have to be anxious about *anything*. That is wonderful news! No fear or anxiety that we have is too small to be beneath God's notice. Encourage your teens to bring all of their anxious thoughts before the Lord and to entrust their worries to Him.

NOTHING WE DO IS OUTSIDE OF GOD'S KNOWLEDGE AND POWER.

God's hand is over *everything* in our lives—the major pains as well as the minor discomforts. He oversees everything we experience and is able to redeem it all. Romans 8:28 says, "We know that for those who love God all things work together for good, for those who are called according to his purpose." If your teens commit to going to an event and later find out about another one that seems like it will be more fun, encourage them to remember that God is working all things together for good—the good of *every*one and *every*thing, not just them. So rather than looking at what they might be missing, help them see the bigger picture and keep their eyes open for how God is working in small ways.

Psalm 139 tells us that God knows us personally and intimately. In verses 5 and 6, David says, "You hem me in, behind and before, and lay your hand upon me. Such knowledge is too wonderful for me; it is high; I cannot attain it." It's incredibly comforting to think that God cares so much about the details of our lives. If He is that involved, we don't need to live in fear about every decision we make. He knew, for instance, that your kids would be invited to the first event before they heard about the "cooler" one.

NEVER JUDGE A BOOK BY ITS COVER.

Okay, that exact phrase isn't in the Bible, but the principle is. In one of their YouTube videos, the School of Life (a nonreligious self-help organization)

"FOMO's favorite weapon is comparison. It kills gratitude and replaces it with 'not enough.'"

—BRENÉ BROWN

emphasizes that people who live out of a FOMO mindset tend to view the world as falling into a dichotomy of lame events/people and exciting events/people.[20] Vulnerability and courage researcher Dr. Brené Brown explains, "FOMO's favorite weapon is comparison. It kills gratitude and replaces it with 'not enough.'"[21] If we are firmly entrenched in this way of thinking, we will judge people by how they appear to us and by what we think they can do for us. We will avoid people who seem boring and unattractive to us. If we judge people by how they *seem*, we're doing exactly what James warns us against in James 2:1 when he says, "Show no partiality as you hold the faith in our Lord Jesus Christ, the Lord of glory."

He goes on to say, "If you really fulfill the royal law according to the Scripture, 'You shall love your neighbor as yourself,' you are doing well. But if you show partiality, you are committing sin and are convicted by the law as transgressors" (James 2:8-9). Just as we really don't know whether a particular event will be enjoyable or disappointing, we have no idea what people are really like simply from their appearance. And even if they do consistently bore us, Jesus wants us to show the same love and respect to every person because He Himself loves all people equally.

The School of Life also points out that people who have a wiser perspective recognize that, yes, it is possible to have some really neat and unique experiences in life, but they also "doubt that the obvious signs of glamour are a good guide to finding them."[22] The reality is that most people and situations have some mix of good and bad qualities, no matter what they look like at first glance.

We can combat FOMO by being grateful for what God has graciously given us, even if it's different than what we envisioned.

BE THANKFUL!

It's easy to focus on what we don't have. There will always be something we want or believe we need. And there will always be much in our lives for which we can be thankful. First Thessalonians 5:18 says, "Give thanks in all circumstances; for this is the will of God in Christ Jesus for you." In Philippians 4:11, Paul writes, "I have learned in whatever situation I am to be content." FOMO focuses on what we do not have. We can combat FOMO by being grateful for what God has graciously given us, even if it's different than what we envisioned.

HOW CAN I HELP MY KIDS NOT TO BE CONTROLLED BY FOMO?

ON THE SURFACE, FOMO promises that we will maximize our lives, our fun, our happiness, our coolness if we don't miss anything—and therefore don't miss the best. Ultimately, it promises a way to achieve abundant life and true joy *without Christ*. But if we're honest with ourselves, giving in to FOMO actually accomplishes the opposite: we're less happy, full of regret, constantly wishing for more or better, never able to really enjoy anything. We become enslaved to our own fear. That's because nothing has changed. Like Adam and Eve, we, too, must recognize that "there is a way that seems right to a man, but its end is the way to death" (Proverbs 14:12). As Jesus said, "The thief comes only to steal and kill and destroy; I have come that they may have life, and have it to the full" (John 10:10, NIV).

So what can we do to combat FOMO and truly live once again? How can we give control of our hearts and minds back to Christ as we teach our kids to do the same?

1. FIGHT FOMO WITH JOMO.

We will actually get more out of life if we embrace the reality that we can't experience everything and if we are grateful for what we *can* experience. Some have termed this the "joy of missing out," or JOMO. It "encourages us to embrace the pleasure of choosing what we want to do (or not do), in a way that engages and fulfills us."[23] Rather than looking at missing out as a failure or something to be avoided, JOMO teaches us to accept our reality and learn to revel in the moment, no matter what it brings. You can do this as a family by helping your kids pick a

Rather than looking at missing out as a failure or something to be avoided, JOMO teaches us to accept our reality and learn to revel in the moment, no matter what it brings.

limited number of after-school activities or by choosing the number of nights per week your family will commit to activities. Then designate the nights you're not out doing stuff "device-free" nights (do an activity or play a game together instead!), and make time to thank God together for all He has given each of you.

2. TALK ABOUT QUANTITY VS. QUALITY.

FOMO also teaches us to believe that the quantity of our experiences is much more important than the quality of them. And yes, quantity is of some importance—just not as much as we've been led to believe. Instead, let's teach our teens to view the *quality* of interactions as highly important too. In fact, it's somewhat of a balancing act. Most of us would not choose to only have one high-quality experience a year; that's just not enough to soothe our God-given desires for adventure, community, and fun. But at the same time, most of us would not choose to have 365 low-quality experiences per year, either; we'd be worn out, overstimulated, and frankly dissatisfied.

So how do we find the right balance? Take time to sit down as a family and look at a calendar. What big things do each of you want to do over the next year? Write them *all* down, using numbers to rank them in order of importance. Then figure out what is feasible to do in the coming year and schedule these activities. The ones that don't make the cut this year can just go on the waiting list for the future, giving everyone something to look forward to. The same can be done for smaller-scale activities. Going through this process together as a family is important because it teaches everyone (including younger children . . .

and ourselves!) to accept our limits and learn to healthily maximize our time.

3. HAVE HONEST, ONGOING TALKS ABOUT FEAR.

Simply telling someone not to fear anymore doesn't usually work. Our kids need help learning to identify their fears (admitting them out loud is powerful!), as well as to recognize when one of those fears has reared its ugly head and is threatening to take over. We must offer them easy steps to follow in those situations. If they recognize they're overcommitted because of FOMO, they need to know they can talk to us about it without fear of being judged or criticized. We also have to pray with them for God to overcome their fear and give them peace. Then we should teach them how to gracefully and kindly back out of some of their commitments, while also helping them identify activities that truly help them rest and rejuvenate.

4. ELIMINATE OR LIMIT SOCIAL MEDIA USE.

We mentioned earlier that a lot of people in Gen Z are getting off social media because of the stress it creates. If your kids have a serious dependence on a certain social media platform, help them evaluate why that is and whether it might not be better to get rid of it, even if only for a time. We talked to a teenage girl who knew she had a problem with Instagram and decided to give it up for a while. Even though she realized it was stressing her out, she had no idea that she would feel as relieved as she did once she took a break from it.

Another option is that your kids could move their most-used social apps to the back page of their phones so that they don't see them immediately upon unlocking the screen.[24] Other helpful tactics include not charging devices in bedrooms at night, turning off app notifications, only checking apps periodically, and setting screen-free times as a family.

5. LEAVE SPACE FOR CHANGING YOUR MIND.

It's possible for us to react so strongly against FOMO that we go too far in the other direction and start believing that it's wrong and flaky to ever change our minds. In her book *Screens and Teens*, Dr. Kathy Koch advises parents to let their kids know that it's not a sin to change their minds. They should still practice an overall pattern of saying what they mean, of course, but they don't need to live in guilt or fear of ever going back on a decision.[25]

6. TEACH GOOD DECISION-MAKING.

Dr. Koch encourages parents not to give kids unnecessary choices and recommends that parents limit their kids' choices when possible.[26] Parents can also help their children by giving them guidance on how to make wise choices. Consider questions such as how the choices will impact them in the long run and how to evaluate preferences against more serious factors. Making decisions is something we all have to do on a regular basis, so help your kids understand that it's better not to put off that responsibility. You can also benefit your kids by helping them figure out what they like and who they are so they can use that knowledge when considering their options. You might even try doing a Bible study with them on the topic of choices, desires, and contentment.

When it comes to wanting to hang out with their friends but not being able to afford doing so, teach your kids how to stay on a budget and encourage them to be honest with their friends if they can't afford an activity.[27] In those situations, your kids could suggest a different activity that's either free or costs less. But if everyone else still decides to do the more expensive activity, that's a great time to be extra aware of your teen's feelings, making sure to praise them for choosing wisely and maybe even rewarding them in a small way.

7. GIVE THEM CLEAR BOUNDARIES.

Part of helping your kids make good decisions about what they will and will not do is to raise them with healthy boundaries. In their book *Boundaries: When to Say Yes, How to Say No to Take Control*

Learning to make age-appropriate decisions helps children have a sense of security and control in their lives.

—HENRY CLOUD AND JOHN TOWNSEND

of Your Life, Dr. Henry Cloud and Dr. John
Townsend write:

> Children begin life in a helpless,
> dependent fashion. Godly
> parenting, however, seeks to
> help children learn to think,
> make decisions, and master their
> environment in all aspects of life.
> This runs the gamut of deciding
> what to wear in the morning to
> what courses to take in school.
> Learning to make age-appropriate
> decisions helps children have a
> sense of security and control in
> their lives.[28]

In Genesis 1, God gives Adam and Eve
real authority to steward the world He
made. This includes making decisions

that impact that world, for better or worse. It's a noble and serious responsibility. The more you can help your kids recognize this responsibility and give them wisdom in exercising it, the better they will be able to avoid FOMO.

8. HELP THEM DO SOME SELF-ANALYSIS.

Suggest that your kids do a self-evaluation in order to see how bad their FOMO is.[29] You can help them with this using the discussion questions section below.

9. THEN DO YOUR OWN SELF-ANALYSIS!

We have to be aware of the example we're setting for our kids. Are we constantly checking our phones? Are we multitasking so much that we're not giving our kids or other people in our lives our full attention? Are we overcommitting to events and responsibilities? How do we handle times when we need to wait and have patience? Are we able to be joyful in those moments? Are we setting an example of how to wait on God? The more we model healthy behaviors, the easier it will be for our kids to pick up those behaviors.

CONCLUSION

THE MAN WE INTERVIEWED who used to be sleep-deprived in college still struggles with FOMO. What's different now, he says, is that it's not ruling his life anymore. The same is true for the woman we mentioned at the very beginning of the guide who used to frequently check AIM. She now has a much healthier grasp on her reactions when she feels like she's missing out. She tries to have good boundaries so that she doesn't overcommit to social events. She does her best to stick to her commitments and reminds herself that God is sovereign over her decisions. When she feels like her friends are deliberately excluding her, she tries to remind herself of the truth (her friends care about her, they wouldn't intentionally make her feel bad, etc.). She also asks for feedback from people she can trust who can tell her objectively if she is overreacting or if she has a good reason to be upset.

Our teens don't have to let FOMO control them. With our help, they can learn to rule their fear, rest in God, be proactive stewards of their domains, and really enjoy the experiences they get to have and the people they have the privilege of knowing.

RECAP

- FOMO, the fear of missing out, is powerful because it's built on exclusivity and it exploits the very human reality that we can only be in one place at a time.

- Because of it, we overspend, are never satisfied, and constantly look for the greener grass. But that can cause us to never commit to anything or to overcommit in the hopes that we can cheat our finite reality. Yet we never give anything our full attention.

- Social media often exacerbates the problem by exploiting our physical limitations and unceasingly putting what we're missing on display.

- FOMO can be made worse by preexisting mental illness and an overwhelming number of choices. It can also lead to recklessness and the development of mental illness.

- The term FOMO is never mentioned in the Bible, but God's Word has a lot to say about it: We should live not from a spirit of fear. We should be thankful for what we do get to experience. God made us finite on purpose (and that's a good thing!). Wanting something so badly we'll do anything for it is idolatry.

- It's possible to help your kids have JOMO! Talk about valuing quality over quantity, help them set smart limits on social media, model wise decision-making and boundaries, and teach them to honestly evaluate themselves on a regular basis.

The term FOMO is never mentioned in the Bible, but God's Word has a lot to say about it: We should live not from a spirit of fear.

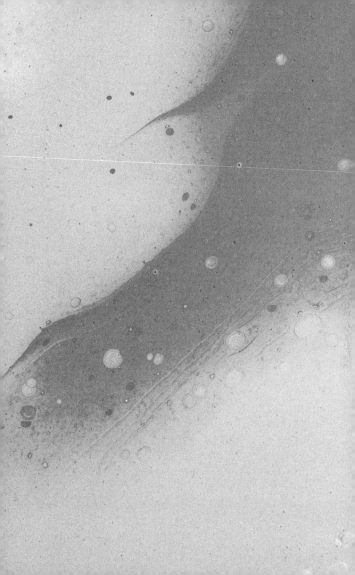

DISCUSSION QUESTIONS

1. Do you struggle with FOMO? If so, how can you tell?

2. How has it impacted the way you feel?

3. How has FOMO impacted your social life? How has your FOMO affected your friends?

4. Do your friends have FOMO? If so, how has it affected you?

5. Is what you're choosing to spend your time on really worth what you're giving up?

6. Do you think social media makes your FOMO worse? Why or why not? How does peer pressure contribute to it?

7. How do you think your life would change if you gave up social media—or maybe just certain

platforms—even if only for a certain amount of time?

8. How can you strike a balance between the quantity and quality of your friendships and activities?

9. What does living a FOMO-free life look like, in your opinion? Do you think it's possible to live that way?

10. How can God's Word guide you on how to deal with FOMO?

11. Have you ever experienced being fully present in something you were doing? If so, what was it like?

ADDITIONAL
RESOURCES

1. *Boundaries with Kids* by Henry Cloud and John Townsend

2. *Boundaries with Teens* by John Townsend

3. Center for Humane Technology: https://www.humanetech.com/

4. "Here's What Happens When You Evaluate Students by Gratefulness and Materialism": https://www .bakadesuyo.com/2010/07/what -happens-when-you-evaluate -students-by-gr/

5. "New Neuroscience Reveals 4 https:// www.bakadesuyo.com/2015/09 /make-you-happy-2/

6. "Be More Successful: New Harvard Research Reveals a Fun Way to Do It": https://www.bakadesuyo.com/2014 /09/be-more-successful/

7. "The Science of FOMO and What We're Really Missing Out On," *Psychology Today*, https://www.psychologytoday.com/us/blog/ritual-and-the-brain/201804/the-science-fomo-and-what-we-re-really-missing-out

8. Check out axis.org for more resources, including *The Culture Translator*, a free weekly email that offers biblical insight on all things teen-related

NOTES

1. "How to Deal with the Fear of Missing Out (FOMO)," Life Coach Directory, September 20, 2021, https://www.lifecoach-directory.org.uk /memberarticles/how-to-deal-with-the-fear -of-missing-out-fomo.

2. "Social Theory at HBS: McGinnis' Two FOs," *The Harbus*, May 10, 2004, https://harbus.org /2004/social-theory-at-hbs-2749/.

3. Patrick McGinnis, "How to Dump FOMO in 2018," *Patrick J. McGinnis* (blog), January 16, 2018, https://patrickmcginnis.com/blog/how -to-dump-fomo-2018/.

4. Deep Patel, "What Gen Z's 'FOMO' Means for Marketers," *HuffPost*, August 19, 2017, https://www.huffpost.com /entry/what-gen-zs-fomo-means-for -marketers_b_5998646be4b02eb2fda32063.

5. David Stillman and Jonah Stillman, "Move Over, Millennials; Generation Z Is Here," SHRM, April 11, 2017, https://www.shrm.org /resourcesandtools/hr-topics/behavioral

-competencies/global-and-cultural
-effectiveness/pages/move-over-millennials
-generation-z-is-here.aspx.

6. Tim Devaney, "Nearly 40% of Millennials
Overspend to Keep Up with Friends," Credit
Karma, April 5, 2018, https://www.creditkarma
.com/insights/i/fomo-spending-affects-one
-in-four-millennials.

7. Sherry Turkle, *Alone Together: Why We Expect
More from Technology and Less from Each
Other* (New York: Basic Books, 2011), xliv.

8. Philip Galanes, "The TikTok FOMO Is Real,"
New York Times, August 27, 2020, https://
www.nytimes.com/2020/08/27/style/tiktok
-teen-fomo.html.

9. Eric Barker, "This Is the Best Way to Overcome
Fear of Missing Out," *Time*, June 7, 2016,
https://time.com/4358140/overcome-fomo/.

10. "Why We Feel FOMO (Fear of Missing Out)
and What to Do about It," SCL Health,
accessed March 2, 2022, https://www
.sclhealth.org/blog/2019/03/why-we-feel
-fomo-and-what-to-do-about-it/.

11. "Social Theory at HBS."

12. Barry Schwartz, "The Paradox of Choice," filmed July 2005 at an official TED conference, TED talk, 19:24, https://www.ted.com/talks/barry_schwartz_the_paradox_of_choice.

13. Dana Dovey, "Fear of Missing Out, FOMO, Is Real, and Could Be Detrimental to Your Mental Health," Medical Daily, October 14, 2016, https://www.medicaldaily.com/fear-missing-out-fomo-real-and-it-could-be-detrimental-your-mental-health-401321.

14. Marina Milyavskaya et al., "Fear of Missing Out: Prevalence, Dynamics, and Consequences of Experiencing FOMO," *Motivation and Emotion* 42 (2018): 725–37, https://link.springer.com/article/10.1007/s11031-018-9683-5.

15. Texas A&M University, "FOMO: It's Your Life You're Missing Out On," *Science Daily,* March 30, 2016, https://www.sciencedaily.com/releases/2016/03/160330135623.htm.

16. Patel, "What Gen Z's 'FOMO' Means for Marketers."

17. Betsy Mikel, "Study Reveals Why Gen Zers Are Jumping Ship on Instagram," Inc., accessed March 2, 2022, https://www.inc.com/betsy -mikel/study-reveals-why-gen-zers-are -jumping-ship-on-instagram.html; Oliver McAteer, "Gen Z Is Quitting Social Media in Droves because It Makes Them Unhappy, Study Finds," Campaign US, March 9, 2018, https://www.campaignlive.com/article/gen -z-quitting-social-media-droves-makes -unhappy-study-finds/1459007.

18. Aziz Ansari: Live at Madison Square Garden - Plans with Flaky People | Netflix Is a Joke," YouTube, video, 2:31, March 12, 2015, https:// www.youtube.com/watch?app=desktop&v =_RbMv7HUiO4.

19. "The Most Oft-Repeated Command in the Bible," University Presbyterian Church, December 16, 2009, https://www.upcorlando .org/pastors-blog/post/the-most-oft-repeated -command-in-the-bible.

20. The School of Life, "Fear of Missing Out (FOMO)," YouTube, video, 3:45, May 18, 2015, https://www.youtube.com/watch?v=VrC _MSG9zSU.

21. Brené Brown, "Don't Let FOMO Kill Your Mojo," BreneBrown.com, https://www.pinterest.com/pin/124412008433455157/.

22. School of Life, "Fear of Missing Out."

23. Michelle Rees, "FOMO vs. JOMO: How to Embrace the Joy of Missing Out," Whole Life Challenge, accessed March 2, 2022, https://www.wholelifechallenge.com/fomo-vs-jomo-how-to-embrace-the-joy-of-missing-out/.

24. McGinnis, "How to Dump FOMO in 2018."

25. Kathy Koch, *Screens and Teens: Connecting with Our Kids in a Wireless World* (Chicago: Moody, 2015), 141.

26. Koch, *Screens and Teens*, 142.

27. Devaney, "Nearly 40% of Millennials Overspend."

28. Henry Cloud and John Townsend, *Boundaries: When to Say Yes, How to Say No to Take Control of Your Life* (Grand Rapids, MI: Zondervan, 1992), 188.

29. McGinnis, "How to Dump FOMO in 2018."

PARENT'S GUIDES
BY AXIS

It's common to feel lost in your teen's world. These pocket-sized guides are packed with clear explanations of teen culture to equip you to have open conversations with your teen, one tough topic at a time. Look for more parent's guides coming soon!

BUNDLE THESE 5 BOOKS AND SAVE

DISCOVER MORE PARENT'S GUIDES, VIDEOS, AND AUDIOS AT AXIS.ORG

www.axis.org

CP1805